Contents

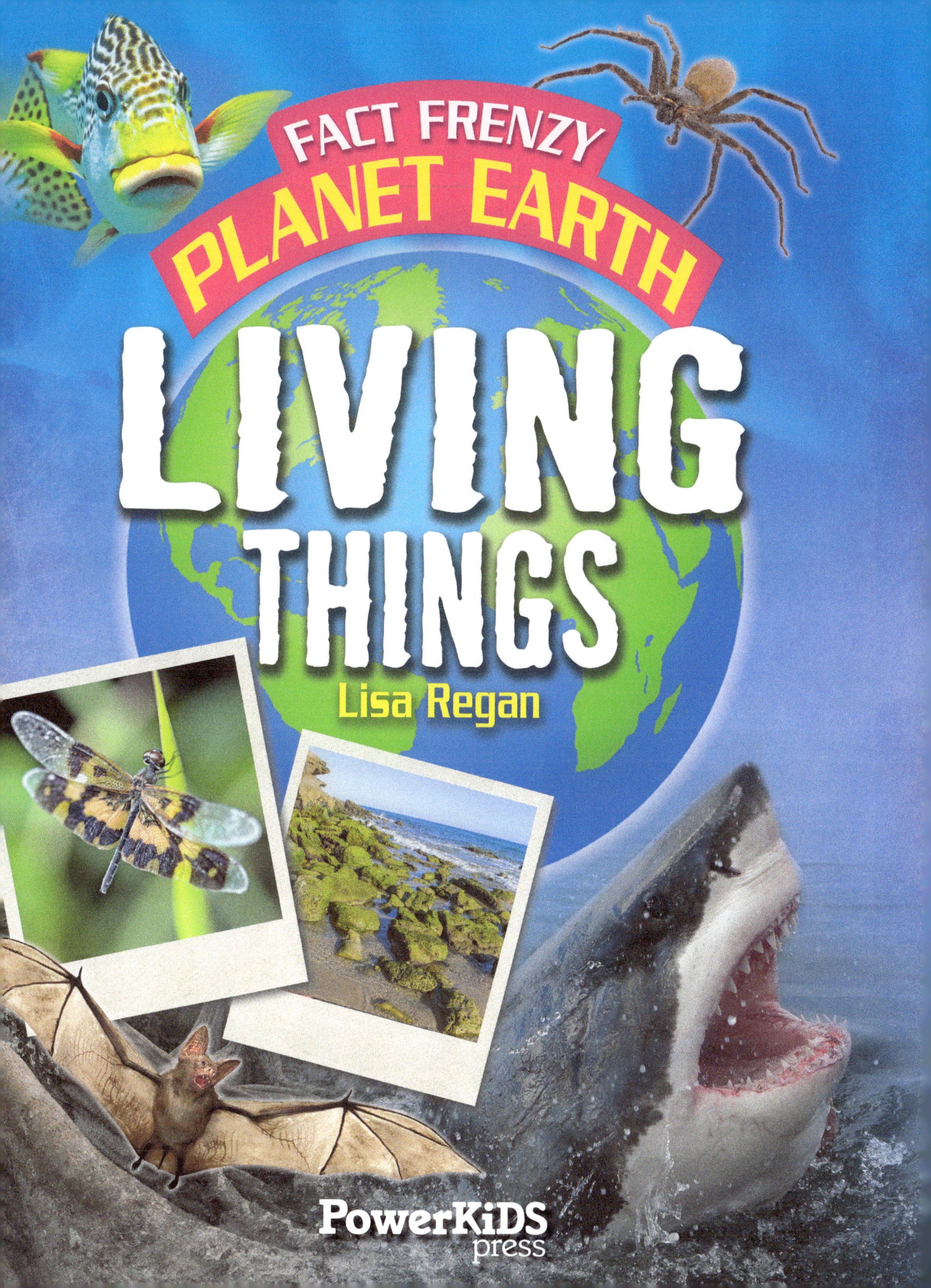
FACT FRENZY
PLANET EARTH
LIVING THINGS
Lisa Regan
PowerKiDS press

Published in 2020 by **The Rosen Publishing Group, Inc.**
29 East 21st Street, New York, NY 10010

Cataloging-in-Publication Data

Names: Regan, Lisa.
Title: Living things / Lisa Regan.
Description: New York : PowerKids Press, 2020. | Series: Fact frenzy: planet Earth | Includes glossary and index.
Identifiers: ISBN 9781725395558 (pbk.) | ISBN 9781725395572 (library bound) | ISBN 9781725395565 (6 pack)
Subjects: LCSH: Life (Biology)--Juvenile literature.
Classification: LCC QH309.2 R43 2020 | DDC 570--dc23

Manufactured in the United States of America

CPSIA Compliance Information: Batch CSPK20: For Further Information contact Rosen Publishing, New York, New York at 1-800-237-9932.

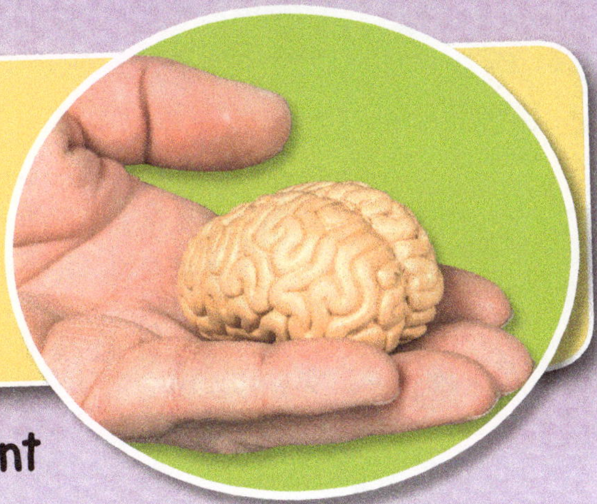

FACT 1 BREAD IS MADE WITH FUNGUS!

Yeast is used as a live ingredient in bread to fill dough with gas bubbles and make it rise. Yeast is a type of fungus, a microscopic, single-celled organism that divides and multiplies to reproduce.

Simple or complex?

Living things come in many shapes and forms. At their most complex, they are breathing, feeding, moving animals, or respiring, photosynthesizing plants. Simpler organisms are classified into three other groups: fungi, prokaryotes, and protists. Scientists differentiate these groups by their appearance and actions, but also by the way their cells are designed. They estimate that over 5 million species of fungi exist on Earth.

FUNGUS IS INJECTED INTO CHEESE SUCH AS STILTON OR GORGONZOLA TO MAKE IT TURN BLUE.

FUNGUS CAN BE SEEN ON THE SURFACE OF ROTTEN FOODS BUT HAS ROOT THREADS THAT INVADE MUCH DEEPER.

Breaking down

Fungi cells have a nucleus and membranes. The group includes yeast, mildew, and toadstools and mushrooms. Unlike plants, they cannot make their own food. Instead, they mostly feed on dead plants and animals, breaking them down to help them decompose. The fungi then absorb nutrients through their cell walls. Fungi reproduce by spreading spores through water or the air.

Almost invisible

Bacteria and blue-green algae are examples of prokaryotes. Their cells have no nucleus but do have a membrane, or cell wall. They are often microscopic, but some examples can be seen, such as the green algae coating on the bark of a tree. Although bacteria cannot be spotted with the naked eye, they can be found everywhere, from rocks and soil to your skin and your computer mouse.

Microscopic misfits

Protists are a strange collection of organisms that do not fit into any other category. Their cells also have a nucleus and membrane, but protists are much, much smaller than fungi, with only a single cell each. Some can cause deadly diseases. Some resemble animal cells, such as an amoeba, which can change shape and move around. Amoebas eat by surrounding food with their body.

Most algae are protists and grow in the water.

FACT 2 YOU CAN HEAR BAMBOO GROWING

Bamboo is the fastest-growing plant in the world. It can reach 100 feet (30 m) high, and has been recorded as growing nearly 4 feet (1.1 m) in a single day. Sometimes it makes a popping sound as the shoots get taller.

Plant life

Plants cannot move to find food, like animals do, but create their own sustenance through a process called photosynthesis. Some rare examples no longer do this, but are parasitic instead and feed on other living things. Generally, plants have roots, leaves, and the stem or trunk. They can be giant trees, or tiny fronds such as duckweed. Mosses and ferns are plants, as are all of the fruits, vegetables, and grains that we eat.

The sap of the maple tree can be made into maple syrup.

Liquids of life

The roots of a plant collect water and minerals from the ground. Water helps keep a plant stable and upright; you will see a plant begin to wilt and look droopy if it needs more water. Nutrients and waste are moved around in a watery substance called sap. Some trees produce another liquid, called resin. It acts as protection against injury or insect attack.

The sunshine cycle

Plant leaves contain chlorophyll, a green substance that absorbs sunlight. This is used to convert water and carbon dioxide (from the air) into food. Water is drawn up through the stem and reacts with carbon dioxide to make glucose, a kind of sugar. Oxygen is given off during the process, making plants vital to animal life on our planet.

A TREE'S ROOTS PROVIDE WATER AND KEEP IT ANCHORED IN THE GROUND.

Sweet treat

Glucose is used to make new cell walls, or is converted into starch to store for later. Plants also make fats and proteins so they can grow. Plants are at the bottom of the food web. They are known as producers, since they make their own food. Animals are consumers, which means they cannot make their own food but have to consume plants or other animals.

FACT 3 THE DYNAMITE TREE EXPLODES

The sandbox tree, which grows in tropical parts of North and South America, is nicknamed the dynamite tree since its seeds explode at over 160 miles per hour (70 m/second). They can be launched over 100 feet (30 m) from the tree.

A SUNFLOWER HEAD IS MADE UP OF LOTS OF TINY FLOWERS THAT EACH TURN INTO A SEED.

Spreading the seeds

The sandbox tree uses a novel method of seed dispersal, but the seeds are formed in the same way as all plants. Plants reproduce very differently from animals. They make flowers containing both the female and male parts. The male parts produce pollen, which must be transferred to the female parts of another flower of the same species. When the two meet, they form seeds.

FACT 4 The gas plant produces flammable fumes that can be ignited on a windless day!

Choose me!

Pollination usually happens with the help of the wind, or insects and animals. Bees, butterflies, wasps, moths, birds, and even bats land on the plants to feed on the nectar they produce. They brush against the pollen and carry it with them as they visit more flowers. These plants usually have bright flowers with vivid markings to attract lots of pollinators.

Carried on the breeze

Wind-pollinated plants produce lots of light, dry pollen that blows around easily. Many grasses and cereal crops—and trees such as spruces, firs, and pines—are pollinated in this way. Their flowers are often small and dull, with no scent or nectar, since they have no need for showy displays to advertise their wares to passing insects.

Some seeds have small hooks so they get carried around on animal fur.

Location, location

After pollination and fertilization, a flower turns into a fruit. The fruit can be hard, like a nut, or soft, like a tomato or a pear, and contains a seed or seeds inside. The seeds have to be spread far and wide so that new plants can grow away from the parent plant. They can be blasted off, like the sandbox tree, eaten and carried to a new place, or travel by themselves with wings or tiny parachutes.

FACT 5

Hayfever is caused by an allergy to wind-dispersed pollen that floats in the air in huge quantities.

FACT 6

SPIDERS HAVE NO EARS!

Unlike people and many animals, spiders don't have ears with eardrums to detect noise vibrations. Instead, they have sensitive hairs on their legs. Many insects also have different ways of picking up sound vibrations.

Hearing aids

Crickets "hear" with their legs, butterflies with their wings, and flies have miniscule eardrum-like structures on their chest. Some hawkmoths can pick up ultrasonic sounds, like those made by bats, with a tiny sensory organ in their mouth. The praying mantis has only a single "ear" by its back legs, and mosquitoes have hearing organs on their antennae. Ants don't have ears either, but detect sounds as vibrations through their feet.

Talk to the legs, man!

BUTTERFLIES, MOTHS, FLIES, AND BEES TASTE WITH THEIR FEET, NOT THEIR TONGUE!

Vital invertebrates

Insects and spiders are invertebrates: animals with no backbone. Other invertebrate creatures include crustaceans (crabs, lobsters, shrimps), worms and leeches, jellyfish and anemones, squid and octopus, snails and slugs, and centipedes and millipedes. Over 97 percent of all the creatures on the planet are invertebrates. They are extremely important, as they provide food for other creatures, pollinate plants, and dispose of waste.

SCORPIONS ARE ARACHNIDS, WITH EIGHT LEGS, IN THE SAME GROUP AS SPIDERS.

Crazy numbers

The sheer number of invertebrates on the planet is mesmerizing. Compare them to mammals, with around 5,000 species, and birds, with roughly 10,000 species; there are 75,000 species of arachnids, and over a million different types of insects, with more being discovered all the time. Insects are a great source of protein and much easier to farm than cattle, so they may become an important food source around the planet.

Growing up

Many insects have interesting life cycles and go through metamorphosis. Their young look very different from their adult form. A fly starts its life as an egg, and changes into a wriggly maggot before reaching its adult form. A moth changes from egg to larva (a caterpillar), and then into a chrysalis before emerging as an adult with wings. A young dragonfly lives as a wingless nymph that looks more like an alien than a dragonfly!

Adult dragonflies only live for a few weeks.

FACT 7 LION CUBS HAVE SPOTS

Adult lions are known for their beautiful golden coat, but their babies have dark spots until they are around three months old. The pattern helps camouflage them in long grass and bushes.

YOUNG LION CUBS ARE PREYED UPON BY LEOPARDS, HYENAS, JACKALS, CROCODILES, AND OTHER LIONS.

Top cat

Even lions need a form of protection when they are young and vulnerable. As they grow older, they become hunters rather than hunted. They are Africa's apex land predator, meaning that they are at the top of the food chain, eating other creatures but not being eaten themselves. Other examples of apex predators are tigers, polar bears, Komodo dragons, alligators, crocodiles, eagles, killer whales, and many sharks.

Chain gangs

A food chain groups together things that live in a single habitat, and places them in the order of what eats what. Food chains usually start with a producer (see page 9), most commonly a plant. Herbivores eat these plants, and carnivores eat the herbivores. A simple example is a rabbit that feeds on grass, and in turn provides food for a fox.

Tipping the balance

Many food chains can exist in a single habitat, and link together to form a food web. The producer is still at the bottom, but will provide food for several creatures, which in turn are eaten by a variety of others. The balance can be delicate. If the plants are in short supply, because of drought or humans clearing the land, the herbivores may move or starve. This leads to less food for the creatures higher up the web.

FOOD CHAINS OFTEN END WITH A SCAVENGER OR INSECT THAT EATS THE BODIES OF DEAD PREDATORS.

Taking in toxins

Other factors can interfere with the food supply. Pesticides, fertilizer, toxic waste, and pollution may enter the food chain at the bottom, and work their way up to the top in larger and larger amounts. Tiny sea creatures called plankton absorb chemicals such as mercury. Small fish eat large amounts of plankton, and become food for bigger game fish such as tuna. When humans eat the contaminated tuna, the mercury levels are higher, and it can make people seriously ill.

Tuna are large, fast apex predators.

FACT 8 OVER 430 PARASITES LIVE ON HUMANS

A parasite is a creature that lives on, or inside, another creature. It gets its food from its host (the creature it lives on), sometimes causing harm, but sometimes hardly noticeable at all.

Finding a home

Human parasites include nasties such as head lice, fleas, roundworms and tapeworms, and mosquitoes. They can trigger a rash or itchiness, cause sickness and diarrhea, or lead to deadly diseases. Mostly, a parasite will feed off its host without killing it. Some parasites use their host as transport or as a breeding ground. They can get into the body through contaminated food or water, or from infected animals.

NITS ARE THE EGGS OF HEAD LICE AND MUST BE REMOVED BEFORE THEY HATCH.

This creepy, woodlouse-like parasite feasts on the blood of its host (the fish).

MALARIA, CAUSED BY THE PLASMODIUM PARASITE, HAS KILLED MORE PEOPLE THAN ALL WARS AND NATURAL DISASTERS COMBINED.

Itch-hikers

Humans are not the only hosts for parasites. Many other creatures have smaller creatures living in their fur, on their skin, or in their gut. You can see this for yourself if you have a pet. Pet owners should be particularly careful that their dog or cat does not catch fleas, ticks, or lice, as all of these love to drink blood. Pets should also be treated against worms, which can make them and their owners ill.

Living together

Two species that interact closely are said to be symbiotic. Parasites rely on their host for food in a relationship that is harmful to one party and beneficial to the other. Cuckoos are an example of a different type of parasitic action. They lay an egg in another bird's nest, and let the mother do the work of hatching and feeding the cuckoo chick.

Here to help?

Some symbiotic relationships can be one-sided, helping one party without harming the other. The barnacles you see on the side of whales do not offer any benefit to the whale, but enjoy a free ride into plankton-rich waters for feeding. Other relationships work both ways. Pollinators (see page 11) get food from flowers, and help the flowers with fertilization in return. Certain birds stay safe and hitch a ride on large herbivores, and eat insects that may bite the animals.

FACT 9 FISH CAN SUFFOCATE IN WATER

Fish breathe oxygen, but they take it from the water rather than from the air. Water is forced out across their gills, and the oxygen dissolved in it can be absorbed into the fish's blood. If too little oxygen is available, the fish will suffocate.

FAST-MOVING WATER CONTAINS MORE DISSOLVED OXYGEN THAN SLOW OR STILL WATER.

Oxygen levels

The amount of oxygen dissolved in water is much lower than that available from the air. Different species need different amounts to breathe: crabs and oysters that feed on the ocean floor, for example, need less dissolved oxygen than fish swimming in the shallows. The oxygen can enter the water as a by-product from photosynthesis (by seaweed and plankton) or be mixed in by waterfalls and waves.

An algae bloom shows up as green scum on the water.

Sailing the seas

Invasive species are a problem in all habitats. Introducing non-native plants and animals disturbs nature's balance and can wipe out established creatures. Large ocean liners have huge ballast tanks to keep them steady in the water. They fill and empty these with ocean water as they travel, carrying new species halfway around the world and spilling them into fresh habitats, causing much concern for oceanographers.

Hotting up

Warm water carries less oxygen than cold water, and scientists are concerned that the average temperature of the oceans is rising. Fish risk suffocating in these warmer areas, unless they swim to other places, damaging the livelihood of local fishermen and disrupting the food chain (see page 15). Shellfish are also affected: increased carbon dioxide in the water prevents them from building their hard, protective shell, leaving them vulnerable to predators.

Plant problems

All sorts of pollution can lower the amount of oxygen available to aquatic creatures. Some rivers are tainted with herbicides (weed killers) that destroy aquatic plant life. The dead plants decay and use up the oxygen in the water, leaving it unfit for fish and other creatures to live there. Other rivers are flooded with fertilizer, causing large algae blooms that deplete oxygen and kill fish.

FACT 10

ELEPHANTS AND HYRAXES ARE RELATED

They may look totally different from each other, but the small, furry hyrax shares its family tree with the enormous, wrinkled elephant. They are also related to the manatee, which spends its whole life in water.

Spot the difference

Scientists find new creatures and plants every year, and try to place them in categories according to their similarities and differences. They also check the characteristics of known creatures to see how they are related to each other, and sometimes revise how they are grouped. Elephants and hyraxes both grow giant incisor teeth to form tusks (in contrast to other animals whose tusks are canine teeth), and females, together with manatees and dugongs, have teats near their armpits. These shared traits link them on the animal family tree.

FACT 11

New species are sometimes discovered in museums! Scientists occasionally realize the specimen they are studying is a totally new species.

What's in a name?

The science of naming and classifying living things is known as taxonomy. One of the most famous taxonomists was Carl Linnaeus (1707–1778), who created a system for naming organisms and arranging them in a logical order, with similar items grouped together. His first categorizations included around 12,000 species of plants and animals. Nowadays, scientists have named roughly 2 million species.

FACT 12

Carl Linnaeus recognized that bats were mammals and not birds, but he classified them as closely related to monkeys!

Dying out

New discoveries are made every year: hundreds, maybe even thousands, of creatures that were previously unidentified. However, species become extinct all the time, too. Extinction wipes out all members of a species so that it can never exist again. It happens naturally, but experts are fearful that human exploitation of the planet has speeded up the process by over 1,000 times.

INSECTS MAKE UP AROUND HALF OF THE NEW SPECIES DISCOVERED EACH YEAR.

Splitting up

How are new species discovered? Sometimes, it is simply by looking in new places. Other times, it is by studying the DNA and finding that similar creatures are actually genetically different. This is known as "splitting," and the reverse can also happen. Known as "lumping," some species are linked together when scientists originally thought they were different.

Scientists cannot agree on exactly how many species of lemurs there are.

FACT 13 HUMAN BRAINS ARE SHRINKING

For the first 7 million years of human development, the brain grew, almost tripling in size. But for the last 10,000 years it has been getting smaller again. Are we getting more stupid, or don't we need such big brains any more?

FACT 14 The sperm whale has the largest brain of any animal, but it is only 0.02% of its body mass.

In proportion

The overall size of an animal's brain is important relative to its body size. Elephants have brains four times bigger than a human, but proportionately smaller when compared to their massive bulk. That helps to explain why elephants aren't smarter than people. Human bodies have become a little smaller as we developed from hunter-gatherers (see page 23) to farmers, but our brains are shrinking at a faster rate.

THE HUMAN BRAIN HAS SHRUNK BY AN AMOUNT EQUIVALENT TO THE SIZE OF A TENNIS BALL!

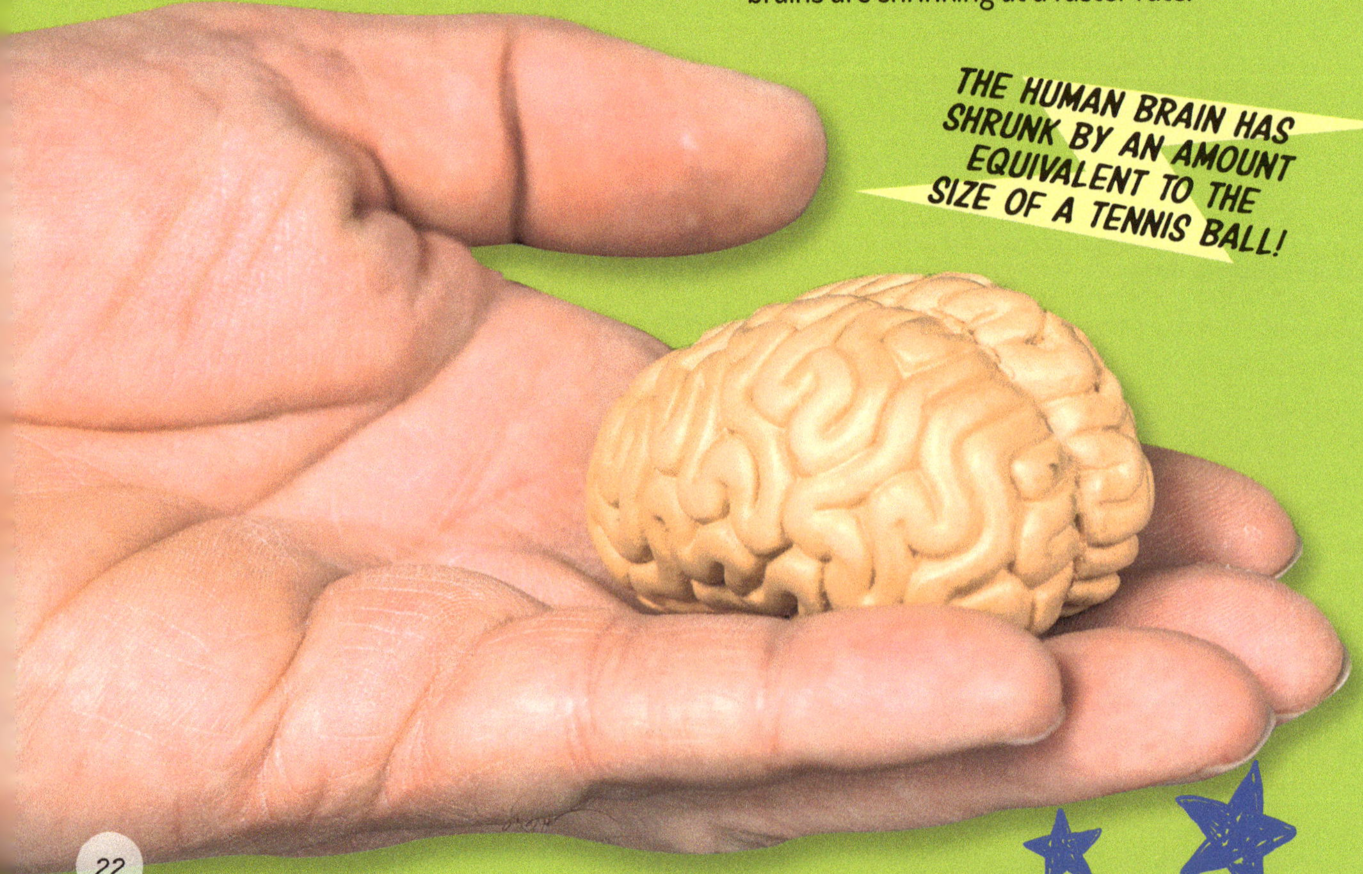

Cave paintings show people hunting thousands of years ago.

Brain food

Some scientists think the brain has become smaller because of our changing lifestyles. Early humans lived a nomadic hunter-gatherer lifestyle, moving from place to place and eating what they could find or kill. They had to use their brains to stay alive, keeping safe from predators and identifying poisonous food. Gradually, different cultures began to settle in one location and grow their own crops.

On the farm

Agriculture developed in many different countries at around the same time. Wild plants were domesticated (chosen for their benefits as food crops) and wild animals were tamed to be useful or kept as livestock. Dogs and sheep were some of the first wild animals to be domesticated by humans, and rabbits one of the last. It wasn't until the Middle Ages, around 1,400 years ago, that people began keeping rabbits for their fur and meat.

The developing world

Towns and cities started to appear, with craftsmen and traders alongside the farmers. People started to own land and build property. Free from the burden of finding food each day, some people became artists, mathematicians, architects, or philosophers. Most early civilizations grew up around freshwater, such as the Nile River in Egypt and the Euphrates River in the Middle East.

FARMING BEGAN OVER 10,000 YEARS AGO AND HAS CHANGED DRASTICALLY SINCE THEN!

FACT 15

The Aztecs and Incas invented peanut butter!

FACT 16 SHARKS ARE EATING THE INTERNET!

Vast lengths of cable stretch underneath the oceans to carry internet signals around the world. Sharks seem to have taken a liking to them, biting their protective casing on the ocean floor!

NEARLY HALF OF THE WORLD'S POPULATION HAS ACCESS TO THE INTERNET, COMPARED TO LESS THAN 1 PERCENT IN 1995.

Shark bait

If the "cloud" of stored electronic information conjures up an image of signals whizzing above your head, then think again. Nearly all of the data that travels around the world does so underwater, along over half a million miles of cable. Telecoms and tech companies have invested a fortune in laying them, and now protect them from inquisitive sharks with an extra-strong outer layer, similar to a bulletproof vest.

There are more internet devices on the planet than people.

Time to talk

Communication has changed so much through human history. Spoken language marks people as different from all other creatures, and allows us to pass on knowledge, stories, and customs. This was done on a small, local scale until the invention of printed books in 1440. Since then, radio, television, and the internet have opened up instant communications between all four corners of the world, informing people about things from far beyond the places they have visited.

Let's explore

The great Age of Discovery in the 15th and 16th centuries was a turning point in the way people saw the world. Navigators set sail to find new ocean routes around the globe, and in the process found lands they never knew about. Those who were fortunate enough to return brought with them foreign foods, and specimens of exotic plants and animals.

Distant shores

Today fast, affordable, long-distance travel has shrunk the world and made it much easier to expand our horizons. Scientists can reach far-flung places to study different habitats. Satellites sitting high in the atmosphere beam pictures into our homes, drones can be sent into inhospitable territory, and geobrowsers show us images of unfamiliar lands without us moving from a desk. The modern, technological world seems a much smaller place.

EVEN MORE FACTS!

You've found out lots about living things, but there's always more to discover! Boost your knowledge with these 10 quick facts.

The word "fungus" is a Latin word meaning "mushroom." The top of a mushroom is called the cap, while the small plates underneath are called the gills.

Reindeer lichen is a fungus that can grow to the age of 100 years. In very cold conditions, it can stop growing and wait until warmer weather returns.

Bees are some of the most important pollinators because they visit many different plants to feed on their nectar. Bees are often attracted to blue and violet-colored flowers.

The giant rafflesia is the world's largest and also the stinkiest flower. This plant relies on flies for pollination, so it smells like rotten meat to attract them.

The praying mantis is a large insect, named after the way it stands holding its two front legs as though it is praying. The front legs have sharp spines that help the mantis catch and hold on to prey.

The great white shark is the largest and most fierce predator in the ocean, and at the top of the ocean's food chain. Its scientific name is *Carcharodon carcharias*, from the Greek words meaning "sharp" and "tooth."

The brightly colored clown fish lives among the stinging tentacles of sea anemones, feeding on the anemones' leftover food. It has a special slimy coat that prevents it from being stung.

The electric eel, which lives in rivers in South America, is named after its ability to deliver a powerful jolt of electricity of up to 600 volts to stun its prey. Despite its name, the electric eel is not an eel, but a species of knifefish.

Hooded seals have the shortest period of suckling of all mammals. Hooded seal pups suckle for only four to five days, but because their mothers' milk is so rich in fat, they double their size during this time.

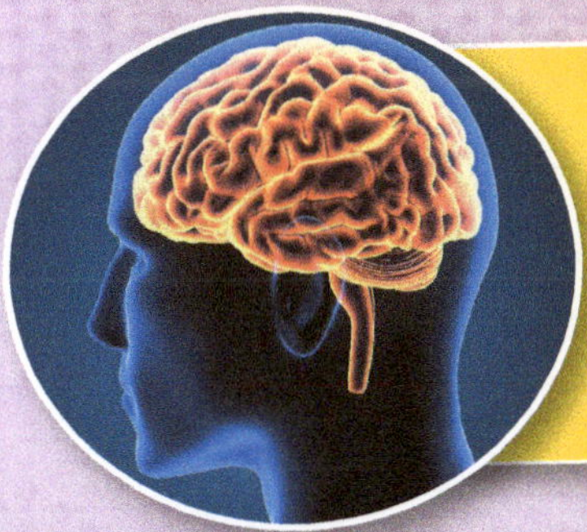

The average human brain weighs 3 pounds (1.4 kg). In comparison, dolphin brains weigh an average of 3.5 pounds (1.6 kg), elephant brains weigh 13 pounds (6 kg), and the heaviest belongs to the sperm whale, at 15.5 pounds (7 kg).

LIVING THINGS GLOSSARY

algae A type of plant with no stems or leaves that grows in water or on damp surfaces.

amoeba The smallest kind of living creature, consisting of only one cell, found in water or soil.

arachnids Members of the class of animals called Arachnida, characterized by simple eyes and four pairs of legs. This group includes spiders, scorpions, ticks, mites, and harvestmen.

atmosphere The layer of air or other gases that surrounds a planet.

bacteria A very large group of microorganisms that live in soil or water, or are parasites of plants or animals.

camouflage The way in which animals escape being noticed by predators because of the resemblance to their surroundings.

carbon dioxide One of the greenhouse gases in the atmosphere that cause global warming.

carnivore An animal that eats meat.

cell The smallest unit of life and basic building block for all living things.

cereal crops Plants such as wheat, corn, or rice that produce grains, which are grown in large quantities for food.

extinct No longer alive.

fertilization The union of male and female gametes, during sexual reproduction, to form a zygote.

food chain A series of living things that are linked to each other because each thing feeds on the one next to it in the series.

food web A combination of food chains, or series of living things that are linked to each other because each thing feeds on the one next to it.

fungus A single-celled organism that divides and multiplies to reproduce.

geobrowsers Three-dimensional, computer-generated representations of Earth or another world.

herbivore An animal that only eats plants.

invertebrates Animals such as insects, spiders, and worms that do not have a backbone.

livestock Farm animals such as cattle and sheep.

membrane A thin layer of tissue that covers or lines an external or internal body surface.

metamorphosis The transformation of a larva into an adult that occurs in certain animals, such as the stage between tadpole and frog, or between chrysalis and butterfly.

mildew A soft, white fungus that grows in damp places.

nectar A sweet liquid produced by flowers, which bees and other insects collect for food.

nomadic Traveling from place to place without a settled home.

nucleus The central part of an atom or cell that controls the characteristics and growth of the cell.

nutrients Substances that help living things to grow.

organism An animal or plant, especially one that is so small that you cannot see it without using a microscope.

parasitic Animals and plants that live on or inside larger animals or plants and get their food from them.

photosynthethis The way that green plants make food using sunlight.

LIVING THINGS GLOSSARY continued

plankton A mass of tiny animals and plants that live on the surface of the sea.

pollen A fine powder produced by flowers that fertilizes other flowers of the same species so they produce seeds.

pollinate To fertilize with pollen.

predators Animals that kill and eat other animals.

proteins Molecules made up of amino acids that are essential to all living things.

sap A solution including mineral salts and sugars that circulates in a plant.

seed dispersal Various methods used by plants to scatter their seeds across a wide area to prevent overcrowding, including using the air, water, and animals.

species A group of plants or animals that share the same main characteristics and are able to breed with each other.

spores Reproductive bodies, produced by bacteria, fungi, and various plants, that develop into new individuals.

symbiotic A relationship in which organisms, people, or things exist together in a way that benefits them all.

tropical Belonging to the tropics, a hot and damp region of the world between the Tropic of Cancer and the Tropic of Capricorn.

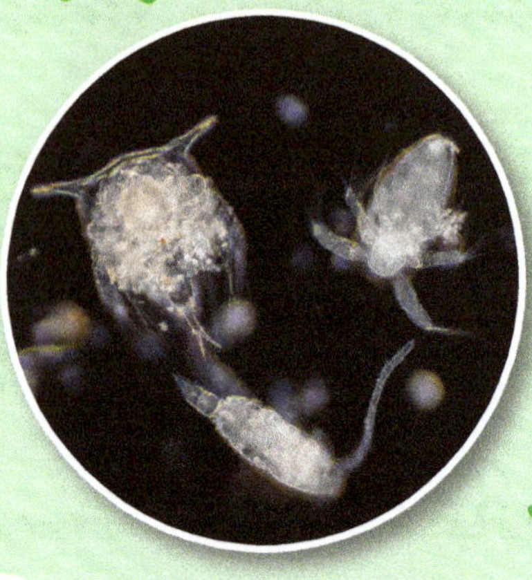

FURTHER INFORMATION

BOOKS

Brake, Mark. *The Big Earth Book*. London, UK: Lonely Planet Kids, 2017.

Cullis, Megan. *The Usborne Book of Planet Earth*. London, UK: Usborne, 2019.

DK. *DKfindout! Earth*. London, UK: DK, 2017.

DK. *Earth: The Definitive Visual Guide*. London, UK: DK, 2013.

DK. *Pocket Eyewitness Earth: Facts at Your Fingertips*. London, UK: DK, 2018.

Gallagher, Belinda. *Wild About Planet Earth*. Thaxted, UK: Miles Kelly, 2019.

MacDonald, Fiona, and Rupert Matthews. *100 Facts Extreme Earth*. Thaxted, UK: Miles Kelly, 2017.

WEBSITES

CoolKidFacts

https://www.coolkidfacts.com/earth-science/

Discover all sorts of facts about planet Earth, from deserts and mountains to the different types of rocks on our planet. Includes simple science experiments and activity worksheets.

Ducksters Earth Science for Kids

https://www.ducksters.com/science/earth_science/

Head to this website to find out all there is to know about planet Earth; you can also try an earth science crossword puzzle and word search!

Science4Fun

http://science4fun.info/earth-science/

Find out more about planet Earth's geology, meteorology, paleontology, and oceanography.

INDEX